IMAGES
of England

ALTON

Bicycle, *c.* 1888. Here we see Bertram Stoodley at the age of about eighteen with his penny-farthing. Born in 1870 he frequently took this machine down Crown Hill with his legs over the handle bars. He died on 27 August 1956.

IMAGES
of England

ALTON

Compiled by
Tony Cross

TEMPUS

First published 1999
Copyright © Tony Cross, 1999

Tempus Publishing Limited
The Mill, Brimscombe Port,
Stroud, Gloucestershire, GL5 2QG

ISBN 0 7524 1572 7

Typesetting and origination by
Tempus Publishing Limited
Printed in Great Britain by
Midway Clark Printing, Wiltshire

Cover illustration: Amery Farm, 1880. Skewering a surplice of hops
before transporting it to the drying kiln.

*I should like to dedicate this book to the memory of Georgia Smith (1925-1997).
A true local historian who shared her skills and knowledge unselfishly.*

Amery Hill, *c.* 1885. A vounteer fire brigade was formed in 1863 with a Paxton manual engine.
The latter was replaced the following year by a Merryweather steam engine, the first used
outside London. The original engine house at the bottom of Amery Hill, seen here, was vacated
in 1891.

Contents

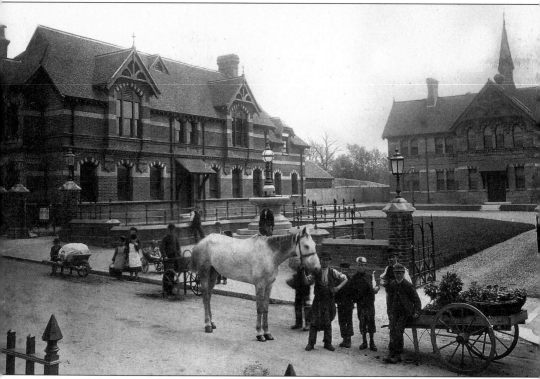

Crown Close, 1882. The Mechanics Institute and the Cottage Hospital on Crown Close two years after they opened.

Acknowledgements

The illustrations in this book, with a few exceptions, are all taken from the photographic collections of the Hampshire County Council Museums Service.

Some originated from family albums of the Curtis, Crowley and Chalcraft families, originally in the Curtis Museum and others are from the bequest of the late C. Hawkins, son of C.W. Hawkins. The remainder have been given or loaned for copying over the years by the good people of Alton to whom I express my sincere thanks.

In the compilation of this book I should like to thank my colleagues at the Curtis Museum and Allen Gallery who have helped in many ways. Special thanks are also due to Wendy Bowen who looks after the photographic collection and who puts up with my incessant requests for prints, negatives or information and sometimes all three at the same time.

Numerous local folk have freely provided information and Jane Hurst has kindly cast a local historian's critical eye over the captions. However, all of the mistakes and omissions are of my own making and I should be pleased to hear of either in due course.

Introduction

THE STORY OF ALTON'S CURTIS MUSEUM

The group of Victorian buildings at the top of Crown Hill, originally the Mechanics Institute and Museum, the Inwood Cottage Hospital and the Assembly Rooms, was achieved in the space of only three years. In the middle of the nineteenth century the railway had created a new boundary in the town, within which were its industries and commercial life; outside lay the fields. At the same time the population was growing and also widening its horizons beyond the traditional daily toil.

Early in 1877 the problems came to a head. The Mechanics Institute had outgrown its premises; the Town Hall was too small to accommodate public entertainments. Miss Bell of Borovere wished to give the town a drinking fountain but there was nowhere to erect it. Money was available for a purpose-built hospital if a site could be found.

In this emergency, Mr Henry Hall offered to present as much of Crown Close and the Crown Gardens as might be necessary. The main condition was that the buildings should be designed by the same architect to harmonize in style and be erected as far as possible at the same time. The designs of Mr C.E. Barry were accepted, and the local firm of J.H. and E. Dyer were entrusted with the building contracts. Work began in 1879.

Patients were transferred to the new hospital on 6 Ocober 1880. On 19 October the Assembly Rooms opened with a 'Dramatic Entertainment' entitled `The Chimney Corner' by the Pickwick Histrionic Club. The following week the Lord Chancellor, the Earl of Selborne, opened the Institute and Museum.

HOW IT ALL BEGAN

The Alton Mechanics and Apprentices Library, to give it its full original title, was founded in September 1837 after some two years of careful preparation. William Curtis, who since childhood had been intensely interested in the world about him, had found some like-minded friends, who derived great pleasure from an evening spent discussing scientific and literary subjects. The movement for Mechanics Institutes was gaining ground in the country and this local group became convinced of the general benefit of forming a society where they could share their interest in the natural sciences with the working men of the town.

By the time the first meeting was convened the idea had won the support of about forty men and a library of more than a hundred books had been collected.

The meeting place for the first two years was a former hop store belonging to Crowley's Brewery, now the site of the Newbury Building Society in the High Street. Most of the lectures were given by John Wright Curtis, William's younger brother, who had just gained his doctor's degree from Edinburgh University. They were both keen naturalists and William's special interest in geology was complemented by John's interest in botany and ornithology.

In 1839 the Institute moved to a more comfortable room which had been built as a ballroom by James Baverstock, and since used by George Saulez as a private school. William Curtis had the help of a committee, and of John Bryant, Alton's postmaster, as secretary.

In 1844 the Institute moved once more, this time to Turk Street to a building provided by Crowleys for the girls of the British School. It was shortly after this that Charles Stewart came to Alton as the new headmaster of the boys British School and together they planned a regular course of lectures which probably helped to secure the future of the Institute. By now the library had grown to six hundred volumes and true to the principle of involving the men of the town, John Gale, a carpenter, was the librarian.

In 1850 in a lecture to the Institute, he suggested the next objective by advocating the educational value of a varied and well-arranged museum. At the end of the year he pursued the point by holding two soirées in his own home at 8, High Street. Ninety eight people saw this private exhibition and it was rated such a success that in the following March, the members combined to stage a similar one at the town hall for the benefit of the Instutute. More soirées followed at the Institute, and then in June 1854, a most ambitious project was organised at the Town Hall, an Exhibition of Works of Art and Industry and of Natural Objects, which lasted three weeks. In addition a remarkable number of people living in Alton lent items. The proceeds of the exhibition were such that the Institute was able to buy 18-20 Market Street.

The members did the conversion work themselves to provide a reading room and library on the ground floor and a year later a museum on the first floor. Local geology played a major part, but there were also the skulls of birds and animals and examples of taxidermy. William Curtis's vision of the Institute as an educational society for the people of Alton had been achieved, and it flourished. The Mechanics Institute was by now part of the life of the town which made it possible to raise the money for the new museum by subscription and the sale of the house in Market Street. A year after the opening, William Curtis died and the new museum was renamed in his memory.

The Alton Urban District Council (AUDC) became responsible for the museum from 1918 and, following the 1944 Education Act, it passed to the Hampshire County Council who have maintained and developed it for the people of Alton since then.

One
Around the Town

Anstey Road, 1887. 'The longest day of 1887 Tuesday, June 21 was a day whose remembrance will long be cherished by the people of these islands.' Thus began a report in the *Hampshire Herald* three days later. This is the triumphal arch of foliage by the Queen's Head on the edge of the town.

Alton Station, 1958. Alton joined the railway age on Wednesday 28 July 1852 some three years after the line had reached Farnham. The station was this impressive stone building. However, the extension of the line to Winchester in 1865 resulted in a re-alignment of the track and a new station, the present one, was built.

No. 51 Normandy Street, 1887. John Tokely, a baker and grocer of the East End Stores, was a newcomer to Alton in 1880. His shop, together with the Star public house next door, were re-developed around 1911 as Enticknaps garage. At this time Orchard Lane, now York Mews, renamed following the Duke of York's wedding in 1986, ran down the side of the garage, then turned right and continued along past what is now the police station to Kingsmead.

Lock's Alley, Normandy Street, *c.* 1935. The alleyway formerly ran down the side of the Congregational Church. The pillar on the left can also be seen on page 50. Sixty years ago visiting artist Fred Ireland painted a number of watercolours of old buildings in the town. His 1936 view of this location with its attractive timber-framed buildings, since demolished and now part of Orchard Lane, is to be seen in the Curtis Museum.

Normandy House, 1867. This was the home of Abraham Crowley (1796-1864), who purchased Baverstock's Brewery on 28 August 1821. The old uneven footpaths of flint and cobbles seem to have been replaced by the new herring-bone brickwork pavements, a little of which survives today in Church Street.

A sale notice, 1892. Following the death of Charlotte Crowley in 1892, Normandy House was sold. It was acquired by the Mechanics Institute for £1,700 as they were bursting at the seams at the Museum just along the road. The formal opening, by the Earl of Selborne, took place on 3 October 1893. However, it gradually became apparent that the place was too expensive to maintain and it was sold in 1898.

Normandy House, *c.* 1890. The gardens behind Normandy House were extensive. In the summer months, fetes and other attractions were often held there. Much later they provided rear access for vehicles to the premises and in 1998 they were built over. The subsequent development of nine cottages was named Rodger's Court, after a family who lived in adjacent Nether Street.

Normandy House, 1956. By this time the house had been divided into two shops, their separate identities being all too evident here. Next door, since December 1945, was the *Hampshire Herald and Alton Gazette* which changed its name to the *Alton Gazette* in 1966. As a consequence, the *Alton Mail* changed its name to the *Alton Herald* in the same year. The façade of Normandy House survives today as the Model Railway Centre and Tandoori Restaurant. The grocery shop of Chanin and Harris is now Sparky's Electrical Centre.

No. 3 Normandy Street, 1900. The family butchers shop of Alfred Mugridge opened in 1899. The site later became Alton Autos and later still, the Crown Hill Garage which closed in 1985. The Little Green Dragon bookshop now occupies the site, following a re-development which was completed in 1994.

No. 10 Normandy Street, 1913. These premises were long associated with a butcher's businesses until 1981. It is currently Goodeve and Partners, an estate agent.

No. 8 Normandy Street, c. 1925. Until 1908, Henry Cork's Universal Stores, were a distinctive feature of Normandy Street. The site was later used by the Farnham Cooperative Society, and some of the staff are seen here. In 1931, the Farnham Gas and Electricity took over the premises.

No. 6 Normandy Street. The two cottages seen here were formerly the house of Isabella Crowley (1834-1919), daughter of Abraham Crowley, who lived almost opposite Normandy House.

Normandy Street, c. 1977. The cottages seen in the previous picture were converted into two shops and are now reunited as Lloyd's Pharmacy. At some time in the past, the shop front at 8 Normandy Street was altered to the featureless façade of Southern Gas. The shop is currently a bookshop run by the Alton Evangelical Free Church.

Normandy Street and Crown Hill, *c.* 1900. On the left are Rodney House, Hill House, the Curtis Museum and the Assembly Rooms before the view drops down Crown Hill. In the past, Rodney House has been occupied by A.W. Moore & Co. estate agents, the Westminster Bank and, in the 1930s, Simmons Stores. Plate glass windows were added at that time and by the 1960s when it was occupied by a television rental company, this once attractive building bore little resemblance to its original form (see p. 127). Renovation in 1991 restored some of its integrity and it is currently occupied by Holybourne Flooring Ltd.

UNDER THE SETTLED LAND ACT, 1882,

BY ORDER OF THE TENANT FOR LIFE.

ALTON, HANTS.

Particulars and Conditions of Sale

OF A VALUABLE

RESIDENTIAL PROPERTY,

KNOWN AS

"HILL HOUSE,"

Situate in the centre of the Town of Alton,
comprising

A Superior Residence, with large Gardens, Pleasure Grounds, and good Stabling. Also extensive Stabling and Yard, and a

CAPITAL MEADOW,

CONTAINING ABOUT

2A. OR. 22P.,

WHICH

MR. J. ALFRED EGGAR

Has received instructions from C. E. Merriman, Esq., to offer
for Sale by Auction, at the

SWAN HOTEL, ALTON,

ON

TUESDAY, AUGUST 28th, 1888,

At FOUR o'clock precisely,

IN ONE OR THREE LOTS.

A sale notice, 1888. Hill House is the only remaining residence on the High Street, its last commercial use being as Mr Redman's dental surgery. Part of the garden was taken for the inner relief road in 1994 and an associated housing development built at the same time.

Crown Close, 1910. Following the memorial service for King Edward VII in St Lawrence Church, on Friday 20 May 1910, there was a procession to Crown Close where Sergeant Cooper raised the flag. Crown Hill was crammed with an estimated 4,000 people

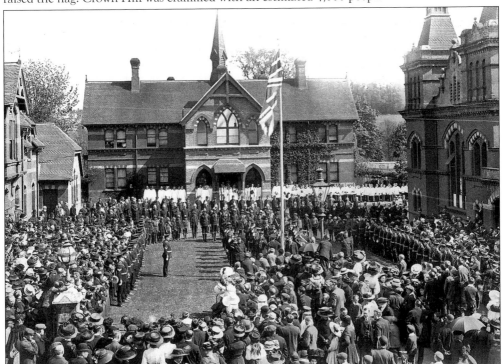

Crown Close, 1910. After the flag had been raised, H.P. Burrell, chairman of the AUDC, read the proclamation of King George V. The band played *God Save the King* and the procession went on to the Market Square.

Church Street, 1911. Thomas Geale, by his will dated 2 May 1653, gave the cottages for the use of people born in Alton. The almshouses are still a charity and are administered by trustees, which include the vicar of St Lawrence. Note the demolition work on the cottages next to the almshouses prior to the building of the Foresters' Hall, currently the Alton Evangelical Free Church.

Vicarage Hill, 1935. The row of cottages at the bottom of the hill were demolished to enlarge the yard at the rear of Kingdon's ironmongers shop. The site is now Kingdon Mews which was developed in 1994-5.

Crown Hill, c. 1920. The buildings on the left include the Castle Inn, which closed in 1971 and the white building next door, 10 High Street, which was Doctor Bevan's surgery. They were successors to the Curtis family practice which had started in 1720.

No. 4 High Street, c. 1920. William Curtis (1836-1924) was one of the seven children of Dr William Curtis (1803-1881) who had founded the museum. He was called curator some time before his father's death and acted in that capacity for the remainder of his life, although his active work stopped in 1914. Part of this garden now forms the garden of the Allen Gallery. The sundial is mounted on a piece of the old London Bridge and still survives today.

Alton banknote, 1815. About 200 years ago Alton had several private banks and some of these were connected with the brewing industry. In 1806, Henry Austen, Edward Gray and William Vincent purchased 10 High Street and operated as the Alton Bank. The premises were sold in 1812 and the bank moved to a building next to Baker's Alley at the bottom of Crown Hill. The bank appears to have failed and Edward Gray was made bankrupt in December 1815.

Crown Hill, c. 1905. The range of buildings on the right side of the road includes the post office which had moved to the brick building on the extreme right of this picture in 1901. The date of the re-building is recorded on the facade. It is still prominent today although the brickwork has been painted.

Crown Hill, c. 1895. The building with the bow-fronted windows on the right is currently occupied by the Rehab Charity shop whilst across the road, the two-storey building with the white front was later rebuilt as the new post office which opened in 1901.

Crown Hill, c. 1955. Some sixty years later the buildings are surprisingly similar. The motor vehicles and modern shop signs indicate the period differences.

Crown Hill, 1939. Souter's Hotel was established in 1928 and before that time the premises had a number of different uses, including a school in 1841. The building with the two bay windows to its left, 18 and 20 High Street, had formerly been occupied by Mr Munday, a saddle and harness maker who had gone bankrupt in 1938. These were demolished in 1971 (see pp 125-6).

No. 30, High Street, c. 1870. Hetherington owned these premises as well as the Wey Iron Works, started in 1865 and later a showroom in Normandy Street. Alfred Hetherington was Chief Fire Officer and the fire station of 1891 was adjacent to the iron works at the bottom of Amery Street. In 1918 the ironmongers shop was sold to Kingdon's, the iron works to F.W. Kerridge and the showroom to the Farnham and District Co-operative Society. Kingdon's traded in the High Street until 1986 and after being empty for some years, the site was re-developed and these premises are now a pet shop.

High Street, c. 1930. Much later the buildings to the right of Kingdon's were demolished for the building of Wey River House which includes the present day offices of the *Alton Gazette*. The shop with the sun awning, 24 High Street, closed in 1965 following the retirement of Miss Chapman, whose family had carried on a footwear business there for four generations.

Market Street, c. 1920. All of the right side of this picture of Market Street was re-developed in 1979. On the left side these rather bland shop fronts hide medieval timber-framed structures.

No. 22 Market Street, *c.* 1925. Mr Trickey came to Alton before the First World War to take charge of the town's skating rink at the Assembly Rooms. After the war, he took over Scarrot's china shop in Market Street. The advertisement on the corner of the building proclaims 'The most varied stock in Alton'. Later, it became the Social Security Office. It is currently occupied by an opticians who moved there in 1993.

THE PUBLIC HEALTH ACT, 1875.

ALTON.

WHEREAS the Urban District Council of Alton have applied to the Local Government Board for sanction to borrow sums amounting to £812 for the purchase of the Alton Town Hall and Market Rights and Tolls, and for the adaptation of the Town Hall for purposes of Council Offices; and the Local Government Board have directed Inquiry into the subject-matter of such Application:

NOTICE IS HEREBY GIVEN that W. H. Collin, Esquire, the Inspector appointed to hold the said Inquiry, will attend for that purpose at the Assembly Rooms, Alton, on Thursday, the Nineteenth day of May, 1910, at Ten o'clock in the Forenoon, and will then and there be prepared to receive the evidence of any persons interested in the matter of the said Inquiry.

H. C. MONRO,
Secretary.

Local Government Board,
3rd May, 1910.

Market notice, 1910.

Market Square, c. 1900. One of the weekly poultry sales with the Umbrella Hospital of William Wright, now a craft shop, in the background. In 1919 there were plans to level the Market Square to make it more convenient to hold the market. The white-fronted cottages behind the crowd were demolished in 1926 to make way for a new poultry market. In turn, this was re-developed and opened as Westbrook Walk in December 1989.

Market Square, 1919. Charles Young, an auctioneer and estate agent, held occasional public sales of cattle, in conjunction with the weekly corn market at the town hall in the early years of the twentieth century. Following his death in 1920, the business was purchased by Alfred J. Martin, in 1923. Mr Martin had come to Alton in February 1909, setting up in business at 18 Market Street. He began weekly sales with poultry, game, sheep and cattle. In 1926 the firm became Martin & Wyatt, and three years later, Martin & Stratford. This name continued in the town until 1987 when the business was acquired by the Halifax Building Society.

Market Square, c. 1935. Many of Alton's car parks have names that reflect the property which was demolished to generate the space needed. That is the case with Lady Place in the corner of the Market Square. Originally acquired with the intention of re-housing Alton's library, it was found to be unsuitable. As an extension to the car park, the house and garden were ideal and permission to demolish was given in July 1961. On the 1666 map of Alton this corner of the Market Square was occupied by James Matthews, a maltster; what is now the Wheatsheaf was the former Bailiff's House, by this time a tavern, the Baliwick, later called the Five Bells.

Loe's Alley, 1935. The bicycle leans against the back wall of the building next to the Plough Inn. The re-development of what is now Boots Corner, in 1979, changed most of the area. However, the building of Westbrook Walk ten years later completed the transformation.

Loe's Alley, 1935. The fenced area, the site of 14 Market Street, is adjacent to the newsagent and tobacconist shop of Miss Caesar. The shop has a similar use today, but the gap is now the large concrete parking area for the servicing of Boots and Westbrook Walk.

Amery Street, Market Street, 1936. Here we see alterations in progress to provide additional shop space. On the opposite corner are the premises of Phillips & Son, builders merchants. Next to them down Amery Hill, is the Salvation Army Citadel built in 1891.

Lenten Street, 1906. The property on the right of this view of was owned by John Adams, a carpenter, builder and shopkeeper in the late 1800s. The nearest premises were bought by Mary White at auction in 1901 after Adams had died, and by 1906, were occupied by James Findon. It could be him in the picture. In 1910, together with Alfred Spier, who occupied 11 Lenten Street, they traded as Spear and Findon, Undertakers.

Lenten Street, c. 1925. On the opposite side of the street, were these cottages built about 1830 by William Gold, a bricklayer, who was living in Chawton, in 1828. The two cottages between these and the rebuilt Adlam's bakery of 1897 were owned by Winchester College.

Lenten Street, *c*. 1930. This Aylward postcard shows a leafy approach to the town centre. The building covered in foliage (centre left) was known as Brooklands where William Curtis, the botanist, was born on 11 January 1746. The house had been built in 1702 by Nicholas Gates. Since re-named William Curtis House, it bears the only ADUC plaque ever produced which commemorates Curtis who died in 1799.

No. 7 Cross and Pillory Lane, *c*. 1930. The building in the centre is now jointly used by the Tourist Information Centre, EHDC Presence Office and the Citizens Advice Bureau, whilst those on either side have been re-developed. The building to the left was demolished and re-built as Cross and Pillory House which opened in 1983. That to the right was re-developed, originally as the Job Centre in the 1980s. At one time known as Bawpyns, the centre house is thought to have been built *c*. 1653 by Moses Neave, a clothier. The bay windows were put in around 1866 by Alexander Sayers.

High Street, *c.* 1935. These two snapshots give an unrivalled view of the shops in the centre of town in the 1930s. Mr Monk sold his chemists shop, started in 1804, to Boots in 1931. During building works in July the following year, a panel of medieval painted wall plaster was found and given to the Curtis Museum.

High Street, *c.* 1890. This George Frost photograph gives an interesting perspective on the buildings and shop fronts some fifty years before the two previous views. Note the Trimming name over the shop on the right (see p. 77).

High Street, *c.* 1905. When William Parker Varney took this photograph Caffel & Co., grocers, had recently enlarged their shop. Next door, at 43 High Street, John Emery had taken over what had been Mr Fewtell's tailors shop and opened The Welcome Refreshment Rooms. The tall building on the far corner of Turk Street is the Royal Oak public house. It was sold to Pearson's, an estate agent, in March 1959. The individual with the wheelbarrow on the right might nowadays be called a 'pollution control operative'.

High Street, *c.* 1935. The premises on the corner of Turk Street are thought to have been built in the mid-1840s having previously been a bank, hop store and guard room. This building was the site of the Hampshire Banking Company in 1861, the post office in 1877, Freeman Hardy & Willis in 1905 and then The Home and Colonial Stores.

High Street, *c.* 1917. The German submarine blockade of the Great War resulted in the rationing of everyday commodities. This is evident from the posters in the shop window. With the men at war, the staff are all female including, on the left, Marjorie Walder. Much later Marjorie and her sister Dorothy were affectionately known around the town as 'the donkey ladies'.

Upper Turk Street, 1901. The meadow between Upper and Lower Turk Street was owned by the Crowley family and the children of A.C. Crowley of Highfield kept their horses there. Cedric Crowley took this photograph of his horse jumping hurdles, but it also shows the construction of the brewery tower in the background.

Windmill Hill, c. 1900. It is possible that the windmill was newly established in 1602 but the earliest reference, discovered so far, occurs in the churchwarden's accounts of 1664. The mill seems to have gone out of use in the early 1800s and the adjacent house took on a new role as an ale house. This was one of five closed in 1907 and was renamed Windmill Cottage. Now called Stillions, it gave its name to the adjacent small housing development of 1969-70.

Ashdell Road, *c.* 1900. The work of building the rustic bridge across the road from Ashdell to King's Pond Meadow was undertaken by a Mr Adams who lived at the laundry on the estate with his wife. It was built of 6 inch (15cm) diameter larch trees and belonged to Frederick Crowley (1825-1910). A handwritten note in the family photograph album indicates that it was pulled down in 1911.

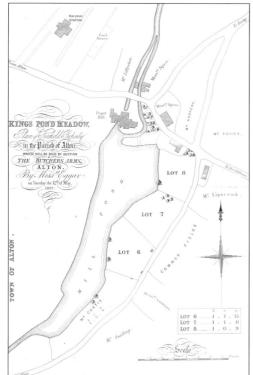

King's Pond, 1857. Originally a general mill with an interesting history, the earliest discovered record of its use as a paper mill is an insurance policy of 1759. William King was tenant in the late eighteenth century and when he left in 1796, John Spicer bought the tenancy.

The Paper Mills, Alton.   VARNEY'S SERIES

King's Pond, *c.* 1905. John Spicer bought the papermill in 1830 and between then and 1860 several other family members were involved. Five years later water power was replaced by steam and at that time 104 people were employed. The mill closed in 1909, but was in use in May 1919 to house German prisoners of war who were working on local farms.

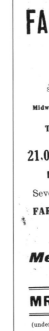

Particulars & Conditions of Sale

of Important and Extensive

FACTORY PREMISES

KNOWN AS

Alton Mills,

At the junction of the Alton, Winchester and Southampton Railway, the Meon Valley Railway, and the Basingstoke Light Railway,

Midway between the Ports of London, Portsmouth and Southampton.

THE BUILDINGS are most substantial,

WITH ABOUT

21,000 Superficial Feet of STORES

MANAGER'S HOUSE,

Several COTTAGES, Engine House

FARM BUILDINGS, Range of Hop Kilns,

and about

17 Acres

OF

Meadow Land & Water

for Sale by Auction, by

MR. J. ALFRED EGGAR

(under instructions from Messrs. SPICER BROTHERS, LTD.)

At the Swan Hotel, Alton, Hants

On TUESDAY, MAY 6th, 1919,

At **FOUR** o'clock p.m.

A sale notice, 1919. The buildings were subsequently acquired by the Alton Battery Company. They had a flourishing sports club with a team in the local football league (see p. 95), a cricket eleven and a tennis club. The works closed in 1958 and were used first by Victoria Foundries and later by Beacon Packaging. Fire damaged the buildings in 1983 and the site was cleared five years later for a housing development.

Moreland Hall, *c.* 1931. Originally built as Ashdell for Frederick Crowley in 1872, it became known as Moreland Hall, a private clinic run by Sir Henry Gauvain from 1925 until his death twenty years later. Gauvain came from Alderney and at the age of twenty eight was appointed to Lord Mayor Treloar Hospital when it opened in 1908. AUDC purchased the house and King's Pond in 1972 and when the pond was renovated as public open space, it earned them the Alton Society John Ambrose Award in 1981. The former clinic site was subsequently developed for housing (see p. 122).

High Street, 1897. The corner site that is currently occupied by Boots looked rather different in 1897. Decorated here for the Diamond Jubilee of Queen Victoria, G.H. Castle had taken over the drapery business of Horace Holman in April 1888.

High Street, 1910. H. Charman acquired the business of J.W. Castle in April 1909. He in turn was followed, sometime before 1915, by Bernard Johnson who was born in 1887 in North Dakota, of British parents, but subsequently returned to the United Kingdom. Later the site became known as Johnson's Corner (see p. 118).

High Street, c. 1865. This very early view of the town gives an interesting impression of the High Street in the mid-Victorian era before it was re-paved with the distinctive herringbone brickwork. Apart from the near buildings on the left and right, many of the other buildings are still recognisable today.

High Street, *c.* 1911. A view similar to the previous one, but taken some thirty years later, shows the re-development on the left of the street. There are new shop fronts on the right and an extra storey on the Royal Oak Hotel.

High Street, *c.* 1931. The re-development of the rather attractive double-fronted house known as Bulbecks, after Richard Bulbeck an occupier of the site in 1398, resulted in the Woolworth building that opened in July 1933. The shop is currently occupied by Homestyle, whilst Smeed and Smeed is now Porter's book and card shop. To the right is Monk's Place, named after an association of Robert de Monck with the site in 1360. The present building is occupied by the Baker's Oven and Eric Morgan & Son who moved here from Market Street in January 1995.

High Street, *c.* 1950. The Mortara family were the last to occupy the whole of 64 High Street which they had bought in 1924. The site is typical of most medieval town centre plots being long and thin. Whilst the front of the site had been re-built in the nineteenth century, the rear comprised a sixteenth century timber-framed building. This was restored as a house in 1995 by the Alton Building Preservation Trust which had been founded three years earlier.

High Street, 1893. Alton's post office has been located in a number of different buildings around the town. In February 1890 it moved from the corner of Turk Street, currently occupied by the Alton Fish Bar, across the road to 72 High Street. This is next to Lansdown House, home of the Midland Bank since October 1958. Chalked on the post box is 'Royal Wedding Day 1893'. On 6 July 1893 the Duke of York married Princess Mary of Teck. In 1910 the couple became King George V and Queen Mary.

High Street, *c.* 1895. Between 1816-9 Swarthmore House, 59 High Street, was the home of the Newman family. Mr Newman seems to have been associated with Baverstock's Brewery at a difficult time for it was sold in 1821. His son, John Henry (1801-90) became an Anglican vicar, but in 1830 joined the Catholic Church, later becoming a Cardinal. John Newman spent his school holidays here and the building, now occupied by an estate agent, bears a plaque to this effect.

High Street, 1906. Nos 65-67 High Street are currently the site of Woolworth's, but in January 1906 it was the Constitutional Club and headquarters of the election campaign for W.G. Nicholson of Bentworth Hall. On Thursday, 25 January 1906 he polled 96 more votes than his Liberal rival and became MP for the Petersfield Division of Hampshire for a second time. Alton had 1,369 registered voters at that time and 1,207 voted, a turnout of 88 per cent.

High Street, 1932. John Albert Hayden (1869-1940) owned two bakers and grocers' shops in the town. One was on the corner of Normandy Street and Nether Street and was acquired in 1907. This is now a hairdressers. The other, seen here in July 1932, was in the High Street next to the Methodist Church. It was later occupied by Mr Shipley until the lease ran out in 1968 (see p. 118). This and adjacent properties were redeveloped in the late 1970s and the site is currently occupied by the Somerfield supermarket.

High Street, 1920. J.A. Hayden's staff included Charlie Carr, seated on the extreme right, who was father of Reg (see p. 54) who later worked there too. Mr Hayden, who was closely associated with the Methodist Church, retired in 1938 and died in December 1940 aged seventy-one.

Butts Road, 1887. The Duke's Head decorations for the Golden Jubilee of Queen Victoria were quite spectacular. In Alton Tuesday, 21 June 1887 started with a peal of bells at an early hour. At 10.30am a parade 'headed by a capital band' marched from the Market Square to St Lawrence Church for a special service. Many of the employers in the town gave their workers a celebratory dinner on Monday evening. Crowley & Co. invited the wives of their staff, however, the women employed at Spicer's Paper Mill received half a crown (12.5p) instead of dinner.

The Fountain from Borovere Lane, *c.* 1905. A newspaper report of October 1879 mentioned that 'Through the munificence of Miss Bell a costly and handsome drinking fountain has been erected at the south-west entrance to the town. It stands by the side of the road where it will fully serve its purpose and evoke the admiration of all that pass by'.

Two
Keeping the Faith

St Lawrence, 1911. Although the church has the appearance of having been built in the fifteenth century, it has a Norman tower and was probably built on the site of an earlier Saxon church. The arches supporting the tower have some attractive Norman carvings.

St Lawrence, 1911. In the twelfth century, the nave was extended to the west and broadened to the north. The old west door, blocked up in 1868, was dated 1180. In the following century the church was extended to the east into what is now the Lady Chapel. Further developments took place as time progressed and in the sixteenth century the present south door and porch were added.

St Lawrence, *c.* 1900. The 37m (120ft) spire was added to the tower in the fifteenth century. Originally covered with lead, this was removed in 1873 and it was re-covered in oak shingles. In August 1942, the removal of the railings for the war effort contributed to the 112 tons of iron salvage in Alton. The churchyard was levelled in 1957.

St Lawrence, *c.* 1866. Until the restoration of 1867, large galleries extended around the church. One crossed the aisle in front of the altar with its back to the east window.

St Lawrence, *c.* 1866. Between the pew doors in the north aisle, seen here looking west, were small seats for the use of the inmates of the workhouse.

St Lawrence, *c.* 1870. An interior view of the church, looking east, after the restoration.

St Lawrence, *c.* 1899. This shows the chancel with the reredos of 1898 erected by public subscription, with the east window in its full glory before it was damaged during the Second World War.

Butts Road, 1896. The church of All Saints was built in 1873 and consecrated the following year. The tower and spire with three bells were added in 1881.

Tower Street, c. 1908. The expanding part of Alton, that the church was built to serve, was known as New Town. The new streets were built in the mid-nineteenth century on former hop gardens previously owned by Edward Waring. The church clock has the interesting inscription 'The Time is Short' around the top of the face.

All Saints Church, 1911. In the chancel is a stained glass window to the memory of Bishop Samuel Wilberforce. An oak reredos and pulpit were given in 1892 and a chancel screen in 1894.

Vicarage Road, *c.* 1905. A grant of £1,500 was obtained from the Ecclesiastical Commissioners and Queen Ann's Bounty towards the cost of a vicarage for the new church. It was built by the Revd Causton who came to the church in 1877. The inset shows Revd Francis Sumner who was vicar between 1892-1912. The building was demolished in 1968 when Vicarage Road was extended to Borovere Lane.

The vicar and choir of All Saints, *c.* 1895. This group is interesting as all their names are known and a number of them were associated with the Wash House Club (see p. 71). The vicar is Revd Sumner, who moved to Chawton in 1912, and the cross bearer is Ernest Gardener.

Church Street, 1965. The Quaker Acts of 1661 and 1664 banned all public meetings other than those of the established church. Despite persecution, Alton's Quakers continued to meet in secret and set up in 1672 what seems to be the second oldest Meeting House in the country. After the Act of Toleration of 1689 life became easier and the Quakers were able to meet undisturbed and finally rest in peace in their own burial ground.

Normandy Street, 1909. The Congregational Church was opened on 14 April 1835 following an interesting history of the group in the town for the preceeding 170 years. An old house in front of the church was demolished in 1845 and the premises extended in 1868. Thirty years ago the forecourt was improved and opened up. The church closed in October 1994 and whilst Knox Terrace was built in 1997-8 on the former burial ground, the future of the main building is still under discussion at the time of writing.

Albert Road, c. 1912. The first Catholic Church was built in a cul-de-sac on the outskirts of the town. Larger premesis were acquired on Paper Mill Lane in 1938 and some twenty eight years later these were re-developed into the present day church. The premises in Albert Road took on a new role as a community hall until they were sold in 1997 for conversion to residential use.

Albert Road, c. 1912. The interior of the original church was plain but functional and could seat a congregation approaching 100 people. The Roman Catholic Bishop of Portsmouth, the Rt Revd Dr Cotter, came to perform a confirmation service on 19 May 1912 and read a message from His Holiness the Pope. At that time the church was said to be 'recently built'.

High Street, c. 1910. After meeting in a number of premises around the town for three years, a site for a Wesleyan Chapel was eventually acquired. The corner stone was laid on 2 October 1845 and the opening service took place on 5 March 1846.

High Street, c. 1906. The Sunday school which was formed around the time the church opened, figured prominantly in the scripture examinations of the Sunday School Union 100 years ago. As the Sunday school head off on an outing, J. A. Hayden in his boater walks ahead of the Mission Brass Band with Charlie Carr (1876-1950) playing the horn next to him.

Church Lads Brigade, c. 1907. The All Saints Sunday School and Parish Rooms, later the infant school and currently the Register Office, were also used as the headquarters of the Church Lads Brigade started by Reginald Crowley in 1895. Founded nationally some four years earlier, it was organized on semi-military lines with the object of training boys in health, citizenship and the principles of the Church of England. The movement suffered as the popularity of the Boy Scouts increased and it seems to have disbanded locally around the time of the Great War.

The Boys Brigade, 1938. Founded in Glasgow in 1883, the movement reached Alton in 1938. A talk on 28 February at the Congregational Church hall was followed by the enrollment of sixteen boys the following week and a company based at the church was started. It seems that the Boy Scouts were at a low ebb at this time and this accounted for the success of the new uniformed group. The officer on the right of this procession almost opposite the church in Normandy Street, is Captain C.W. Hawkins, previously a scout leader.

High Street, c. 1960. In 1886 a gallery was built at the High Street end of the Wesleyan Chapel. It was supported by two iron pillars and the front consisted of fifteen square-boarded panels. The last service took place on 28 March 1976, but it was not until September 1979 that the foundation stone of the new church was laid. The service of opening and dedication took place on 6 September 1980.

High Street. Reg Carr (1911-1996) was a well-known Altonian. At one time he worked for Mr Hayden in his High Street grocers shop and later ran the Upper Froyle Post Office and Village Store. He served on the AUDC in the 1950s and 1960s and had a keen interest in the Methodist Church. He is pictured here in October 1979, with a 'time capsule' built into the foundation of the new Methodist Church.

Three

On the Land

Will Hall Farm, *c.* 1900. Mr Berry Knight sits on the shaft of a horse-drawn wagon.

Will Hall Farm, *c.* 1900. Mr H. Merrett, seen here, died at the age of ninety-three on 11 November 1920.

Will Hall Farm, *c.* 1900. Mr John Bush, hurdle-maker, enjoys a breather.

Will Hall Farm, *c*. 1900. Mr
Arthur Munday milks the cows

Will Hall Farm, *c*. 1900. Wagons and poultry in the rickyard.

Will Hall Farm, c. 1900. Hop kilns.

Will Hall Farm, c. 1900. Transferring hops from a basket into a surplice out in the hop garden.

Will Hall Farm, *c.* 1900. Packing the kiln-dried hops into a pocket using a hop press.

The functional smock was popular working wear for agricultural labourers in Hampshire, especially to the east and south-east of Winchester from the 1780s, right through the nineteenth century. Indeed, smocks persisted among shepherds and milkmen in some rural areas of Hampshire until the 1930s. The farmers and carters of the county were prime wearers of such smocks as functional over-clothes, which protected them from the dirt, cold and rain associated with their outdoor jobs.

Hop picking near Alton, 1895. Picking began in late August or early September depending on the hops and lasted four or five weeks. The additional labour was provided by home pickers, townies, Londoners, gypsies and travellers. The local school holiday was timed to coincide with hop picking but as the potato harvest followed, school attendances could be rather erratic at this time of year.

Hop picking near Alton, 1924. Three generations of the Albury family working in the hop gardens on Wilsom Road. These were in production until the early 1980s but are now built over as part of the industrial estate. The earnings from this seasonal work was often used for buying winter shoes for the children and in the days before families could afford holidays, the late summer hop picking was a healthy outdoor alternative.

Hop picking near Alton, 1922. The Revd Samuel Chinn ministered in the villages of Kingsley, Shortheath and Selborne from 1861-1894. In 1868 the Hop Pickers Mission became recognised helping the 10,000 people who came into the Farnham, Petersfield and Alton districts for the hop picking. There were many changes after the Second World War and 1956 saw the use of mechanical pickers for the first time. The work of the mission subsequently declined.

Mill Lane, 1950s. Before the industrial estate was developed Mill Lane was a country lane leading to Anstey Mill Farm and the nearby Anstey Mill. The farm and the old mill are still recognizable in the middle of the modern warehouses which are linked by wide roads with busy traffic.

Mill Lane, 1950s. Anstey Mill farmhouse is thought to date from the sixteenth century although it has been much altered over the years.

The remains of the adjacent mill pond today bear no resemblance to this idyllic view of some fifty years ago with children in a punt.

Four
Schooldays

Anstey Road, 1911. Under a Trust Deed of 21 March 1638, John Eggar of Crondall, founded a Free School near Alton. He died on 20 March 1641, the school charter was signed by Charles I in September and the school opened in 1642. Since then there have been twenty three headmasters and the current head teacher, Mrs F. Martin, took up her post in September 1997.

Anstey Road, late nineteenth century. Headmaster Mr S.J. Poole and his pupils are seen outside the original Eggars School building which is to be converted for residential use. There were 32 on the roll in the early 1900s and the number had risen to nearly 400 in 1969 when the new school in London Road, Holybourne was officially opened by Dr the Rt Hon. Horace King, MP on 12 July 1969.

Church Street, *c.* 1905. The Dean and Chapter of Winchester, owners of the rectoral tithes of Alton, by deed dated 25 January 1841, granted to the vicar of Alton and others, the yard and buildings belonging to the rectory, in perpetuity as a school for poor children. The last surviving trustee in 1857 vested this property, the National School, now St Lawrence School, in the vicar and churchwardens of Alton and their successors.

Church Street, *c.* 1891. Following the addition of an extra classroom in 1858, there was supposedly room for 450 children. In 1891 the average attendence was 128 boys, 110 girls and 104 infants. The master was Samuel Mussell who lived next door at Amery Cottage. Miss Court was girls' mistress and Miss Wilcox, who shared the other cottage at the school with her, looked after the infants.

Amery Hill, 1950s. Alton Senior Mixed Council School opened on 17 April 1939 with 391 pupils and 10 staff. The headmaster was Edward Luke. The building which stood on land bought from Amery Farm, took two years to complete and had the latest in electric lights and central heating. Space was always a problem and in 1948, a second storey was added to the north wing. Eleven years later, the south east and west wings received similar treatment. Its title was shortened, first to the Alton Council School, and then with the 1944 Education Act, to the Alton County Secondary School. It became Amery Hill School with the introduction of Comprehensive Education in 1974.

Chawton Park Road, *c.* 1910. The site was acquired by Sir William Treloar in 1907 for his hospital and college for crippled children. As a result of the National Health Service Act, the hospital was taken over in 1948. The Lord Mayor Treloar College moved to Froyle the following year. In April 1972, the Wessex Regional Hospital Board agreed to the sale of about four acres of land at the site for the purpose of building a sports centre, which was opened by well-known boxer Henry Cooper in March 1975. At the time of writing, the future of the former hospital site is a subject of some debate.

Five
People

Vicarage Hill, 1896. The original Fire Station, or Engine House, was a square building at the bottom of Amery Hill (see p. 4). In 1891, the Fire Brigade moved to a new site around the corner in Cut Pound. They are pictured here in the road between what is now the community centre and the library with Brook Cottage in the background.

Julius Caesar, *c*. 1858. William Caesar came to Alton from Odiham about 1840 and for many years was a tower of strength to the Alton Cricket Club. Julius was born on 31 January 1852 and inherited his father's love of cricket. An uncle of the same name was in the All England Team which toured Canada and the USA in 1859. Julius Caesar was known as a hairdresser and as a bugler in the fire brigade. He died in 1927 and was buried on what would have been his 75th birthday.

Sons of William Curtis, *c*. 1850. William Curtis (1803-81), the founder of the museum, married Jane Heath in 1830 and they had seven children. Their four sons were Thomas (1838-65), Charles (1840- ?), William (1836-1924), who wrote *The History of Alton* in 1896, and Arthur (1844-98).

'Our Domestics', 1865. William Curtis was born in 1803 at 4 High Street and he spent the first twenty years of his married life at 8 High Street. On the death of his mother in 1851 he returned to no. 4. The family album included this group taken in the garden.

The Crowley family of Highfield, c. 1900. The Crowleys had connections with many of the other well-known Alton families including Curtis and Chalcraft. The marriage of Gertrude Evelyn, third daughter of A.C. Crowley to H.P. Burrell in 1878, the year after Mr Burrell had purchased the Crowley Brewery, maintained a family presence in the local business.

High Street, c. 1890. Henry Hall bought the Hawkins Brewery in 1841, moved to Alton the following year and built the Manor House on the site of the former White Hart Inn. They had ten children and this is probably their Golden Wedding celebration on 21 July 1890. Born in 1814, he died on 31 January 1899 followed by his wife on 8 October 1906.

Hall's Brewery, 1862. The two breweries in Alton employed people in a range of supporting occupations. In spite of increasing mechanization in the nineteenth century, brewing was still a labour intensive industry involving malting, engineering, bottling, coopering and distribution.

The Wash House Club, *c*. 1894. This unique club was started by Charles Bond (1887-1932), seated centre. Its background was the Church Lads Brigade (see p. 53) in which most of its members served including Ernest Gardener, seated right, who was later the editor of the *Hampshire Herald*. Charles Bond, the second of three brothers, was an apprentice carpenter with the builders J.H. & E. Dyer. He became a Sunday school teacher at the age of fifteen and after undergoing training he was appointed Assistant Priest of All Saints in 1914. He became vicar in September 1921.

The Cox family, *c*. 1895. Joseph Cox, second from the left in the back row, was born in Alton on 14 February 1877. He led an interesting life and at the age of ninety wrote *An Ordinary Working Man's Life Story*. This provides a fascinating account of everyday life in the town.

William Wright and family, *c.* 1905. Another Altonian who recorded his life story was William Wright, born 12 August 1846. He started as a chimney boy at the age of eight and lived a full and eventful life before he died on 29 March 1933. His book *From Chimney Boy to Councillor* appeared when he was eighty five years old. One of his lines is worth recording: 'Good health is better than riches'.

Normandy House, October 1893. The move of the Mechanics Institute to Normandy House was followed by a formal opening by the Earl of Selborne on 3 October 1893. The great and the good of the town are represented here on the Institute Committee including Frederick Crowley (front row, fifth from left) and (to his left) William Curtis, son of the founder of the museum.

The sons of H.P. Burrell, August 1909. Harry Percy Burrell (1853-1938) lived with his family in Brooklands, now William Curtis House, Lenten Street. He had four daughters and four sons, seen here, Charles, Godfrey, Aldwyn and Evelyn.

Assembly Rooms, c. 1918. The twelve councillors of the AUDC and their staff of five are seen here under the chairmanship of Mr A.W. Cox, seated, centre. The council was formed following elections on 15 December 1894 and it replaced the Alton Board which had been founded on 1 August 1860. The AUDC was based initially in the town hall, but in 1934 they moved into Westbrook House and remained there for the next forty years. UDCs were abolished under local government re-organization in 1974 and the East Hampshire District Council was formed. The Alton Town Council came into being at the same time giving the County three tiers of Local Authority.

Anstey Road, 1967. In 1919 Captain Augustus Agar (1890-1968) was awarded the VC and DSO for naval actions in Russian waters. He retired to Hampshire in 1949, living first at Hartly Mauditt before building Anstey Park House in 1963. When his Coastal Motor Boat was *en route* to Southampton it stopped briefly outside the house and he showed it to children from nearby Mayfield School. The preserved vessel is displayed by the Imperial War Museum at their Duxford site near Cambridge.

High Street, 1968. Charlie Hawkins and Peter Brears from the Curtis Museum are seen examining the outbuildings housing the printing equipment belonging to the former King's Library. The author of the *Story of Alton* published in 1973, and much other local history material, Charlie Hawkins had been born and bred in the town and lived here all his life. He died in February 1989 at the age of 81. An oak, the first tree in the Alton Society's 'Trees for Life' scheme in Flood Meadows, was planted in his memory the following May.

Six

Transport

Church Street, *c.* 1880. Henry Munday had been a ploughboy, groom, coachman and chauffeur and spent sixty two years in the service of the Curtis family. He is seen here with his wife and the Curtis family trap in the yard which is now part of the garden of the Allen Gallery. He died in 1974 at the age of ninety nine.

The Swan Hotel coach, *c.* 1890. The hotel operated a coach service to the nearest mainline railway station at Winchfield, near Hook until the railway came to Alton in 1852.

Loe's Alley, *c.* 1890. Edwin Loe, was a grocer, wine and spirit merchant and was on the board of directors of the Alton Gas and Coke Company. He was elected on to the AUDC at their first election in 1894 with 319 votes. He is seen here in the yard behind Bulbeck House on the High Street, the site of the original Woolworths. Born in 1840, Edwin Loe died on 29 March 1924. The building behind the cart is still to be seen adjacent to Loe's Alley today.

Turk Street, c. 1920. The Trimmings had used this property at 2 Turk Street for the last quarter of the nineteenth century before buying it in the early 1900s. A little later, the family also had a chemists shop around the corner in the High Street.

Basingstoke Road, c. 1925. Mr Grace is seen here by the New Odiham Road junction with Basingstoke Road. The toll house was demolished in 1966, the road has been widened and now has a mini roundabout to deal with a higher volume of traffic than seen here.

Cyclist, c. 1890. The solid tyres and vicious looking saddle do not suggest a comfortable ride was had on this machine. In February 1896 the Hampshire County Council considered a resolution that it would be just and desirable in view of the increasing use of main roads and highways by cyclists, that a tax should be imposed on cycles the proceeds of which would be in aid of the highways.

Family cyclists, c. 1895. It is not recorded whether the Crowley family, seen here, of Highfield, Windmill Hill were among the members of the Alton Cycling Club, who had their inaugural meeting in February 1886. The club had a bicycle and tricycle division and ten years later decided to form a ladies section with an annual subscription of 2s 6d (12.5p).

Bath Chair, c. 1895. Jane Curtis (1807-1897), seen here with Nurse Jordan, was one of two unmarried sisters of the founder of the museum who lived in one of the family houses on Crown Hill.

The Butts, *c*. 1910. This aeroplane is a copy of the classic Bleriot, in which the aviator of the same name first flew the English Channel in 1909. It has been suggested that this machine could not take to the air and survive and it is possible that it was a 'mock-up' produced for a local film.

Whitedown Lane, 1899. Work began on the Alton-Basingstoke railway line in September 1898. An embankment was needed to raise the line to cross the valley occupied by Basingstoke Road between Will Hall Farm and its junction with Whitedown Lane.

Whitedown Lane bridge, 1899. Across Whitedown was a deep cutting and Whitedown Lane had to be re-aligned and a new bridge constructed near what is now the end of Kings Road. The new bridge over the Basingstoke Road is seen between the trees in the distance.

Butts Junction, *c.* 1905. A signaling diagram supplied in 1903 in conjunction with a Board of Trade inspection of the new Meon Valley line shows a stage for giving a signal tablet to trains using the three lines out of this important junction. The tablet is seen here being given to a Medstead bound train.

Butts Junction, *c.* 1905. A forty lever signal box was built in connection with the new railway lines in 1901. Following the closure of the line to Basingstoke in September 1932, the layout at the junction was simplified and the signal box became redundant. It closed in February 1935 and only the foundations are visible today by the Butts railway bridge near the French Horn.

Alton Park, *c.* 1909. Following the opening of the Lord Mayor Treloar Hospital and College in 1908 a private platform was constructed. This made it easier for patients to reach the site by train on the nearby Basingstoke and Alton railway that had opened seven years before.

Alton Park, c. 1930. Later the platform was faced with concrete and the wooden staging replaced. The additional rail was necessary because of the sharp curve of the bend. Despite the closure of the line to Basingstoke, coal for the hospital boilers arrived at a special siding that continued in use until 11 July 1967.

Alton station, 1929. With the opening of the Meon Valley line, the station had been enlarged in 1903 by making the right platform double-sided. The branch line service to Basingstoke operated by an 0-4-4 tank engine is seen here leaving platform three on 17 August 1929.

Alton station, 1952. The 4.10p.m. service to Southampton operated by an M7 tank engine is seen about to leave platform two on 25 October 1952. The last steam train to Southampton ran on 3 November 1957 and the last day of service on the line was 4 February 1973. The directors of the railway company had been petitioned by the ladies of Alton in March 1894 for the construction of a covering to the footbridge, seen in the background.

Alton station, 1960. The Railway Enthusiasts Club of Farnborough visited the area on a North Hampshire tour on Saturday 15 October 1960. They used an M7 fitted with Push-Pull equipment and with two carriages and visited the Treloars siding and Farringdon.

Butts Junction, 1966. Between 1965-7 the main line was undergoing major works and it was necessary to close it at times. On Sunday 1 May 1966 the 10.30a.m. Waterloo to Weymouth service was diverted via Alton. Seen here crossing the Butts Bridge at the former Butts Junction, it was hauled by Merchant Navy Pacific locomotive 35008 *Orient Line*.

Alton station, Spring 1961. The appearance of a new Crompton diesel has aroused the interest of three onlookers. The uniformed staff are Sam Willis and Len Hillier, both station foremen. Four of these Class 33 diesels have been preserved on the Mid Hants Railway – one is working and the others are in the early stages of restoration. The signal box, which opened in 1903, closed in September 1980. Following a fire, it was partially demolished in February 1984 and the base can still be seen by the side of platform one.

Steam lorry, c. 1920. Mechanization of transport was the most significant aspect of the development of the brewing industry in the first thirty years of the twentieth century. This Crowley Sentinal steam lorry shows Charlie Rodgers with Mr D. Simpson as driver's mate. In January 1904, the Alton Rural District Council attempted to claim £39 6s 9d against Crowley & Co. for damage to a local road allegedly 'caused by the extraordinary traffic of their steam wagon' which had been acquired two years earlier.

Crown Hill, c. 1912. The two bicycles in the background and the motor cycle and sidecar outside the museum demonstrate some of the changes in personal transport that were taking place before the Great War.

High Street, c. 1927. July 1897 saw the appearance of the first motor car in Alton. The Lutzmann went swiftly and noiselessly down the High Street into the Swan yard before anyone noticed its presence. However, when the news got around it attracted considerable attention and was quickly surrounded by an eager crowd.

High Street, c. 1930. In 1920 there were about 200,000 cars registered in the country; ten years later the figure was a million. Anyone was allowed to drive after obtaining a licence for 5/- (25p) and driving tests were only introduced in 1935. Petrol at this time was 1s 6d (7.5p) a gallon, car tax was 3 guineas (£3.15) and the price of a small Ford car in 1925 was £125. Although it was the start of cheap motoring, motor cycles were still very popular and British built machines dominated the world.

Normandy Street, *c.* 1935. The Duckett family bought Alton House in 1932 after it had been derelict for seven years. It became a popular stopping off point for motorists and coach travellers heading for the South Coast. The hotel developed over the years and was involved in the social life of the town through the activities of Ray Duckett. He sold it in 1985 and retired to Devon where he died in March 1997.

Crown Hill, *c.* 1950. The line of parked cars and vans down Crown Hill seen here were a taste of things to come as personal car ownership began to increase. This was accompanied by a corresponding decrease in public transport starting with the closure of the Meon Valley railway on 5 February 1955.

Butts Road, *c.* 1959. The sawmill in Ackender Road was financed by Miss Crowley and started by a Mr Poore in the 1890s, principally to provide work for members of the Salvation Army. Later acquired by Mr Pearce, it was hit by a stick of stray bombs which fell on the area at the end of September 1940 causing considerable damage. The corner site became Urquharts Garage in 1955 and later Clover Leaf until November 1996. Haven Ford had re-developed the adjacent site in Ackender Road as a petrol station and garage in 1990. In June 1998 Caffyns Ford moved onto the corner and at the present time a housing development is under construction on the former garage site next door.

Amery Street, *c.* 1979. This site of the fire station from 1891 to 1922 became a bus depot in 1932. It was subsequently extended in 1955 and although it was located in one of the town's narrowest streets, it was in service until 1988. The former transport yard opposite, at one time occupied by an old nissen hut (see p. 114), has been re-developed as Fielder's Court.

High Street, *c.* 1960. Congestion in the centre of Alton was brought to an end with the opening of the by-pass on 28 September 1971. Since then town centre traffic has gradually increased and an inner relief road, originally planned in the 1960s, was opened in January 1994. A year later a new traffic management scheme was introduced in the town centre in a further effort to reduce through traffic.

Chawton Park Road, 1972. The railway line to Basingstoke had closed in 1932 although coal traffic had continued to Lord Mayor Treloar Hospital until 1967. The demolition of the railway bridge in Chawton Park Road took place on Monday 20 November 1972 as part of an improvement scheme to provide access for the new sports centre.

Seven

Sport and Leisure

Windmill Hill, 1875. Abraham Curtis Crowley (1823-78) with his wife and ten children by the croquet lawn at Highfield. The house, by the railway bridge on Windmill Hill, was sold in 1910 and later became St Mary's Convent. The site has since been re-developed for housing.

Lynch Hill, *c.* 1910. The walk to Lynch Hill went past Anstey Mill and over the bridge before crossing the stile to get to the tree-covered slope formerly popular with children and courting couples. Although the footpath is still there it is not quite the rural walk it was since the town's industrial estate now occupies the area on the left.

Normandy Street, *c.* 1880. Public Houses had a tradition of sporting teams and the Alton Quoits Club had a court behind the Red Lion pub in Normandy Street. In February 1886, there was a meeting of the Alton Butts Quoits Club at the French Horn at which they agreed to continue, suggesting that the future of the game had previously been in some doubt.

Alton Cricket Team, 1899. Pictured outside the pavilion on the recreation ground, later acquired by Courage & Co. is a largely unknown cricket team. The two young players seated on the ground and the player in the deck chair on the far right are three of the Burrell brothers also seen on page 73.

Alton Bowls Club, c. 1912. In June 1887 there was a meeting of the Bowling Club at the Market Hotel where there was a green. However this group, including William Wright and George Frost, are seen here probably behind the Swan Hotel where the outbuildings and bowling green were converted into a car park in 1960. The Bowls Club moved to the town park in 1954, and the Chawton Park Indoor Bowls Club opened in 1996.

Alton Wednesday Football Team, 1912. The club known as the 'Greens', was composed of players who worked in local shops and could only play on their half-day off. They held a celebratory dinner in June 1912 following the presentation of a shield as winners of the Aldershot & District League. They played 22 matches over the season winning 14, loosing 6 and drawing 2. They scored 83 goals and let in 44 suggesting their defence might have been a little suspect!

Alton Football Club, c. 1905. The early history of football in Alton dates back to 1878 and work is currently in hand to research what promises to be a fascinating story. At present, little is known about this successful football club pictured at what later became Courage's sports ground.

St Lawrence Football Club, 1927. Football in Alton mirrored the national scene with the churches promoting the sport. All Saints, the YMCA and St Lawrence were all active locally and apparently with some success, as this picture suggests.

Alton Battery Company Football Club, 1935. Following a meeting at the All Saints Club room, on Tuesday 22 June 1920, the Alton & District Junior League was formed by the seven clubs who were represented. The Alton Battery Company Football Club became the first club to win the local league and the Harvey Charity Cup in 1930. The ABSC seem to have maintained their success judging by the two cups seen here. Only one member of this team is known, Toby Richardson (back row, fifth from the left).

Boy Scouts, *c.* 1909. The 1st Alton Troop of the Boy Scouts was formed in February 1909. During the First World War they helped guard the local railway lines and German mariners interned at Alton Abbey in nearby Beech.

High Street, 1937. The local celebrations on Coronation Day, Wednesday, 12 May began with an open air service in the Public Gardens. At 1.30pm a children's fancy dress parade assembled in the Market Square and headed by the Town Band, marched to Courage's sports ground. Rain did its best to ruin the day as it had on numerous previous Royal celebrations. As a consequence, the children's sports were postponed for two weeks.

Eight
Military Miscellany

High Street, c. 1895. This column of troops marching through the town are probably on their way back to Aldershot. The impressive building on the left is the Manor House with Henry Hall standing in the doorway. The Manor House was demolished in 1968 and replaced by the building currently occupied by Currys, Powerhouse and Dicksons furniture shop. Part of the former garden (see p. 70) is now a car park.

Carnival, 1900. The outbreak of war with the Boers in South Africa on 11 October 1899 was quickly followed by a number of military disasters. However, the following year saw the relief of Kimberley, Ladysmith and Mafeking and the capture of Bloemfontein, Johannesburg and Pretoria. In Alton, a carnival was arranged for 12 July 1901 with the object of helping the Daily Telegraph Widows and Orphans Fund and £96 was raised for the appeal. There was a parade of floats and this one was entered by Messrs J.H. & E. Dyer. By the end of the war on 31 May 1902 22,000 British soldiers had died in the campaigns, many of them from disease.

Chawton Park Road, 1902. In June 1900 it was reported that Alton had been 'fortunate to be selected as the site of a new Military Hospital Camp to be associated with the casualties from the Boer War'.

Chawton Park Road, 1903. The work began on Saturday 23 June 1900 and the general design of the buildings was by Edward Shield. They were said to be novel in character, practical in design and attractive in appearance. Princess Louise made a number of visits to the site before performing the official opening on 14 June 1903.

Princess Louise Hospital, 1904. The 3rd Company Royal Army Medical Corps eventually occupied the site, but with the ending of the war, there was little need for its facilities and it became surplus to requirements.

Alton Station, *c*. 1900. These two views published by Holliday and Co., photographers of Station Road, Alton, date from the early years of the 1900s. The ladies of the British Red Cross Society are seen collecting by the entrance to the Railway Station and on Paper Mill Lane near the Station, probably for the local hospital. Local trade directories show that Holliday and Co. came to Alton some time in the period 1903-1907, but had gone by 1915.

Yeomanry Carabiniers, 1908. Sid Archer, Willy Tuckett, Harry Adlam and Bert Longman in camp with the Alton & Winchester Troop of the Hampshire Yeomanry Carabiniers. Under the Haldane reforms of 1906-12 the Volunteers and Yeomanry were re-organised into a Territorial Army. This had the primary responsibility for home defence but a secondary role of relieving regular overseas garrisons and providing trained men in the event of a major conflict.

'Some of the Boys', c. 1914. Over 800 men from the town served in the Great War. From the start of the conflict the vicar of St Lawrence, Revd Elvin had kept a roll of honour of those who served in the forces. From 1915 the names of those who died were inscribed on a roll of vellum. At the end of the war this was incorporated into a Memorial Chapel of St Michael and St George in the church.

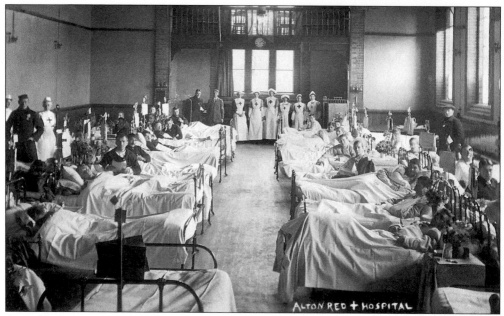

Assembly Rooms, 1914. The people of Alton responded to a request to send clothes to Belgium in August 1914 and the following month a scheme was introduced for offering hospitality to Belgian refugees. A house in the High Street, formerly Conduits Hotel and now occupied by Lloyds Bank, was taken over and at the end of September twenty Belgians arrived.

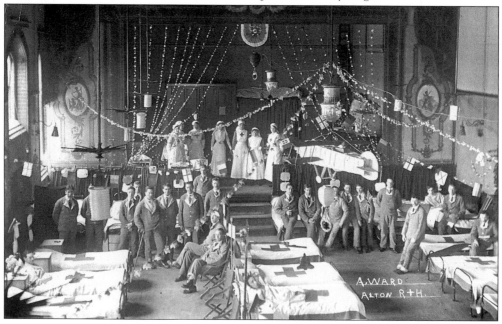

Assembly Rooms, 1914. In November 1914, the Assembly Rooms was turned into a Red Cross Hospital for Belgian wounded and the building stayed as a Military Hospital until January 1919. The First World War which claimed the lives of so many on the battlefield, also profoundly affected the character and the everyday life of the nation back home. It was the first total war and the whole country contributed to the war effort and few survived its effects.

Heath family, c. 1917. The Government was eventually forced to introduce conscription in February 1916, whilst for those left behind, hardships through shortages were common and rationing was eventually imposed in 1917. In this wedding photograph of the Heath family of Prospect Place, Alton, note that few appear happy and the young men present are in uniform.

The Powell family, 1918. No. 49087 Sapper L.J. Powell survived many of the horrific earlier battles on the Western Front and is seen here with his wife and young son in the Spring of 1918. On his return to France, however, he was killed and his name is one of the 169 on the bronze tablet mounted on the Cairn.

High Street, 1919. The Treaty of Versailles officially ended the First World War on Saturday 28 June 1919. A Peace Carnival was held in Alton on 19 July 1919 when all local children were presented with a Peace Mug. Later in the year there was a War Service Reception and Dinner for Alton men returning from the battlefields.

Crown Close, 1920. A War Memorial was the subject of considerable discussion and the chosen design, a Cairn, was eventually unveiled by the Rt Hon. the Earl of Selborne on Hospital Sunday 19 September 1920.

Market Street corner, 1938. The worsening situation in Europe during the late 1930s was evident in Alton as elsewhere, for in January 1938 there was a meeting to discuss air raid precautions and a call for volunteers to assist with them.

Normandy Street, 1938. Part of an exercise to simulate a poison gas attack in the town. What is now the Community Centre was then the assembly and distribution centre for gas masks in the district.

Practising with a stirrup pump, Town Gardens, c. 1940. The task of coping with the effects of an expected devastation was the responsibility of Air Raid Precaution services. Mainly part-time volunteers, who had other full-time jobs, they had to know their area and its residents thoroughly, report exactly where bombs fell, guide fire, rescue, medical and mortuary services to an incident and advise them during the emergency. The service became known as the Civil Defence from September 1941 onwards.

Butts Road, 1940. This group of ARP men are seen outside Fenton's Garage which was next to the Duke's Head. On the left is fire officer, W. Bradley Trimmer, a former town clerk, while the person with his hands on the pump is Harold Carr, later killed in action in France.

Nursery Road, 1941. War was declared on 3 September 1939 and it was not to be long before Alton become directly involved when seven local men died in the sinking of the *Royal Oak* at Scapa Flow on 20 October 1939. Many further tragedies befell the people of the town during the war and the town itself was not spared the effects of enemy action.

Eastbrook Road, 1941. Two bombs fell on Nursery Road and Eastbrook Road at around 9p.m. on 13 March 1941. They caused five deaths, destroyed a house and two bungalows and considerable other damage to the surrounding area.

Eastbrook Road, 1941. Dick ('Binsa') Wells, his sister Nellie, Mrs Finden and two soldiers billeted nearby were killed. It is still possible to see where the bombs fell as the bungalows were re-built in a different style. The site of the house in Nursery Road was cleared, later becoming a playground before Alpha Cottages were built.

High Street, 1944. This Salute the Soldier parade took place on 8 July 1944 when the salute was taken outside Westbrook House by Field Marshall Sir Cyril Deverell accompanied by General Sir George Jeffreys, the local MP.

High Street, 1944. The Guard of Honour at the Salute the Soldier parade was formed by 24th Battalion Hampshire Home Guard. Behind them on the wall of Westbrook House is the appeal 'thermometer'. The week-long savings campaign raised a local record of £255,166. The Home Guard formed on 19 May 1940 stood down at midnight on 31 December 1944.

Cut Pound, 1945. There were many street parties following Victory in Europe Day on Tuesday 8 May 1945 and church bells rang all day, something that had not been allowed during wartime. Buildings were decked with flags, including the Hawkins house, here, by Cut Pound at the bottom of Amery Hill. There were further impromptu celebrations for VJ Day, when victory in the East was announced three months later.

Nine

Since the War

The Butts, 1972. Originally in the parish of Chawton, these cottages were built some time between 1746 and 1829 next to the French Horn public house on the edge of the Butts. At a sale of Chawton Estate land in August 1921 they were sold for £380. They are seen here undergoing restoration in 1972.

Anstey Road, 1972. The parish of Alton looked after the poor in a variety of premises until the workhouse was built in 1793. The Poor Law Amendment Act of 1834 resulted in the Union of eighteen local parishes and a Board of Guardians who administered the premises. It has now been converted to sheltered housing, whilst the site of the 1926 hospital next door, is now part of a housing scheme managed by Brendon Healthcare.

Paper Mill Lane, 1967. Following the First World War, the old paper mill was used by the Alton Battery Company until 1968, Victoria Foundry and later Beacon Packaging. Fire damaged the buildings in 1983 and five years later the site was levelled for the housing development which occupies the site today.

Paper Mill Lane, 1957. Just after children had passed by on their way home from school on the afternoon of Thursday 7 February 1957, a section of the high wall alongside the Catholic Church collapsed into Paper Mill Lane. The wall was thought to have been built in about 1865 when the railway was extended to Alresford. At that time the road was lowered to accommodate the new railway bridge at the bottom of the hill.

Alton Station, 1962. The demolition of Alton's original railway station in June 1962 was hastened when a fire started by the workmen got out of hand. The fire brigade was called and it was soon under control. A wall was pulled down to make it safe, but a huge chimney collapsed without warning. The following week another wall collapsed damaging the nearby Station Cafe and blocking the road.

Amery Street, 1979. Eleven years ago the bus depot was suggested as a suitable site for a much needed new library. The existing building, the old Civil Defence Centre just around the corner, was taken over in December 1968. The library had moved from the town hall where it had first opened in October 1946. The scheme fell through and offices were built which opened in 1992. They are called Barclay House by Travelbag, the current occupants.

Cut Pound, 1971. Recent years have seen the upper reaches of the river Wey tending to dry up in summer months, but in 1971 a strong flow earlier in the year produced an abundant growth of weed and vegetation. Council workmen were deployed in clearance work at Cut Pound, near where the stream flows under Amery Street and what is now the community centre.

Amery Hill, 1971. In early 1971 Len Powell and his wife who had run the corner shop at the bottom of Amery Hill since February 1963, decided to install a new shop window. The work exposed an old sign indicating that at one time the shop had a licence for the sale of Farnham United Brewery products. This brewery had been taken over by Courage & Co. in 1927.

Vicarage Hill, 1967. The early eighteenth-century vicarage at the top of Vicarage Hill was rather large and very expensive to maintain. A new one was built in the garden and the old one, seen here, was demolished in October 1967.

St Lawrence church, *c.* 1969. This aerial view of the area around the church is unfortunately undated, however, it shows the new vicarage of 1967 as well as Amery House, which was demolished in 1975.

Church Street, 1950s. The band of the Alton Salvation Army leads a Royal British Legion parade from St Lawrence Church. The wall of the old vicarage can be seen on the left.

High Street, *c.* 1950. A medieval farmhouse called the Manor House of Flood was re-built in the 1730s and is today known as Westbrook House. It was acquired by Dr Charles Burnett in June 1839 and he established a Private Lunatic Asylum which operated between 1845 and 1915. AUDC bought the house in June 1931 and rebuilt the right side as a new fire station which was in use until 1981. Alton's first purpose-built car park was created behind the building in 1934.

High Street, 1960s. The demolition of 57 High Street opened up a new view of the Watney's Brewery tower. The replacement shop was used by SCATS and is currently occupied by Coral. The little car passing by is a late-1950s Heinkel bubble car.

High Street, *c.* 1963. A large number of properties were demolished to make way for the new Keymarket supermarket which opened in 1979. The store on the corner of Drayman's Way, is now Somerfield. Severe frosts during the winter of 1962 produced large cracks in the corner of the Wesleyan Chapel and it had to be shored up.

High Street, 1979. Following the death of the owner, Bernard Johnson, the draper's shop closed in 1957 ending almost 200 years of trading on the site. The site was excavated inside the buildings in the spring of 1977, in advance of re-development. This picture shows the site before demolition and the building of the new Boots shop which opened in 1980.

Market Street, 1979. Adjacent to Johnson's Corner in Market Street, the former Plough Inn, a timber-framed building, dating from the mid-seventeenth century, was also demolished in 1979 and incorporated into the new Boots building. A pub from about 1840, it closed and was used as a temporary store for the Curtis Museum in the late 1960s.

Market Street, 1979. All of the buildings shown here were demolished in 1979 and the sites re-developed. The imposing structure of Loe's bakery built in 1900, had been occupied by the Co-operative Stores before their new shop was built in the High Street in 1969. The front of the adjacent two buildings, 10 and 12 Market Street, had been altered several times, but inside was preserved a timber-framed structure from the sixteenth century.

Market Square, *c.* 1960. Behind this British Legion parade is the TSB which opened in the town hall on 13 October 1948; later the *Alton Herald* was located here. The town hall, built in 1813, was renovated in 1987 and the enhancement of the Market Square followed resulting in the removal of car parking. The Alton Town Council obtained ownership of Market Square from EHDC on 1 November 1998.

Wootey Estate, 1970. In this view of the new housing development is Wootey Infant School (centre), which opened on 8 January 1968. The junior school, which opened four years later on the adjacent site, is yet to be built. Marlfields is in the process of construction and was officially opened on 3 July 1972, although it had taken its first residents in 1971.

Butts Road, 1975. Built in 1845 on a former hop garden to replace a house in Normandy Street, the original police station cost £1,400. It contained a house for a superintendent, accommodation for a sergeant, three cells and stables. It was enlarged over the years and a magistrates court was added. It was replaced by the new building in Normandy Street-Orchard Lane which was opened by the Rt Hon. Lord Denning, Master of the Rolls, on 29 September 1978. The building seen here was demolished the following year to make way for the new fire station.

Market Street, 1979. The site of Michael Worthington's former barber shop was re-built in 1978 to produce a pleasing result. The lack of a pavement outside the former Plough pub on the other side of Market Street was remedied with the re-development of Boots corner.

Windmill Hill, c. 1975. Until the construction of Wilsom Road in the nineteenth century, Windmill Hill was the route to Kingsley and beyond. So it is not perhaps surprising that it has been a popular vantage point for illustrations of the town. This view of the Watney's Brewery tower from Windmill Hill shows how prominent a feature it used to be on the Alton skyline.

Ashdell Park, 1972. In March 1972, work began to demolish Ashdell House, latterly known as Moreland Hall. In estate agent terminology the grounds became the site of 'a unique development of 55 high quality houses in a delightful parkland setting' and ranged in price from £8,600 - £12,050.

Upper Turk Street, 1975. Built by Crowley & Co. in 1901, the brewery tower was eventually demolished in July 1975. The white building in the photograph has since been extended and a replacement lamp post is in a similar position opposite. The Sainsbury's supermarket of 1992 now occupies the former brewery site. Although the road is still there, it has been blocked by a new roundabout on Turk Street, built to provide easier access for supermarket deliveries.

Kent Lane, 1971. Kent Lane was named after William Kent who owned the site in the mid-nineteenth century. He died in June 1871 and exactly 100 years later, it was agreed to demolish the cottages and barn to provide additional car parking. The brewery tower behind the barn helps locate the site which is now part of the car park in Mount Pleasant. The barn, which had been used as a store for the Curtis Museum, was carefully taken down and re-erected in Lower Froyle the following year.

Turk Street, 1970s. The row of four cottages on the right of Turk Street were demolished for the building of the central section of Drayman's Way, which opened in 1994. With the new road open, the town centre was subject to an enhancement scheme which was undertaken in 1995. The completion of the scheme is recorded on a plaque on Boots shop on the corner of Market Street and High Street.

Cross and Pillory Lane, 1970s. The Warren's Transport buildings to the left of the EHDC's presence office were re-developed in 1982. The unusually-shaped new building, Cross and Pillory House, was designed around a central courtyard which features a three-storey high brick sculpture. Made from 7,560 individually numbered bricks, the sculpture took three months to complete.

Market Day, 1980. The popular market day auctions in the old Poultry Market were conducted by Graham Stratford, a well known local figure. They came to an end in 1987 when Martin & Stratford was acquired by the Halifax Building Society. The site was cleared the following year for the development of Westbrook Walk which opened in 1989.

High Street, 1971. Almost thirty years ago the demolition of two buildings on Crown Hill created access to a new car park at the rear of the former Manor House. At the time of writing, planning permission has been given to build across this entrance. The new design will undoubtedly add to the street scene and it will also plug one of the town's most depressing views – the back of the Manor Park Brewery!

High Street, 1971. The entrance was created in September 1971 by the demolition of a former butchers shop and the adjacent building, previously occupied by the *Alton Gazette*. At the same time the demolition of 18-20 High Street, seen here encased in scaffolding opposite, produced the infamous 'gap site' on Crown Hill.

High Street, 1971. A few days later the effect of the demolition on both sides of the High Street is evident, with an almost clear swathe created from Vicarage Hill through to the back of the then Harp Lager Brewery. Ten years ago planning permission was granted for the building of a supermarket on this High Street site, but the subsequent proposal to build a Sainsbury's store meant that it was not built. The site in the foreground now has almost thirty years' growth of trees on it.

Normandy Street, 1960s. The need for car parking in the 1960s led to proposals to demolish 26-30 Normandy Street. They survived, but thirty years later, the owner, Guy Radford, wished to re-develop the site. The supposed antiquity of the buildings ensured that they were retained and during restoration work in 1996, Elizabethan wall paintings were discovered. As part of the development, a terrace of houses was built at the rear and the scheme was awarded the Alton Society's John Ambrose Award in 1996 for the most praiseworthy addition to the built environment that year.

Normandy Street, 1982. This area has always offered an interesting range of shops providing goods and services on a human scale. Plans for a supermarket on the right ten years ago were thwarted by the Sainsbury's proposal. However, an alternative development on the former garage site providing a mix of retail businesses and housing, has added greatly to the town.

Church Street, 1968. Nos 10-12 Church Street were bequeathed to the Hampshire County Council by W.H. Curtis (1880-1957), and opened as an annexe to the museum in 1963. The gates on the right were replaced by smart doors when the Allen Gallery was renovated in 1977-8. The work included a new exhibition gallery and a pleasant garden at the rear. The building and its new displays were re-opened by Dr Roy Strong, director of the Victoria and Albert Museum, on 13 March 1980.

Crown Close, 1982. Children's holiday activities have been a feature of the Curtis Museum for a generation and the most popular are the practical sessions. At the end of a week of activities in January 1982, Luath Grant-Ferguson, with the cap, arranged a printing session using the Columbia Press, made in about 1860. As he had spent a lifetime in the printing industry, Charlie Hawkins (centre, right) was also particularly interested to see the results of the children's efforts.